BIBLE
KEYWORDING
GUIDE

beyondthehighlighter.com

Copyright © 2019 by Rob Sinclair (Beyond the Highlighter)

IT IS ILLEGAL AND UNETHICAL TO DUPLICATE COPYRIGHTED MATERIAL.

All rights reserved. No part of this publication may be reproduced, stored in a retrieval system or transmitted in any form or by any means - electronic, mechanical, photo- copy, recording, or any other – except for brief quotations in printed reviews, without the prior permission of the publisher.

Bible Keywording Guide logo mark designed by Evangela Creative
Cover design by Chad Landman
Edited by Dawn Weaver – *maidtoedit.com*

Published by Kaio Publications, Inc.
www.kaiopublications.org

Scripture quotations taken from the New American Standard Bible® (NASB),
Copyright © 1960, 1962, 1963, 1968, 1971, 1972, 1973,
1975, 1977, 1995 by The Lockman Foundation
Used by permission. www.lockman.org

ISBN-13: 978-1-952955-01-3

Printed in the United States of America

ACKNOWLEDGMENTS

It is said that we all stand on the shoulders of those who came before us. That is certainly true for the inspiration behind this project. A big thanks to:

Everyone who put up with me talking about this project non-stop. You know who you are!

Shelby Piche, for early layout and format inspiration.

The staff at the Bear Valley Bible Institute of Denver (2012 – 2014), for their love and efforts to cultivate within me a deeper love and understanding of God's Word.

Denny Petrillo, for teaching me his ways, introducing me to key words, and instructing me in just about every concept and method found in these guides.

Dawn Weaver, for her master editing skills and unwavering enthusiasm that refreshed me every time I put pen to paper.

Chad Landman, for taking this project to the next level and believing in the dream.

And most of all, to my biggest fan and amazing wife, Kylie. You've believed in me every step of the way and have embraced the vision that these guides must exist. I love you!

CONTENTS

INTRODUCTION 5
THE EPISTLE OF JAMES 12
STUDYING JAMES 13
   GENERAL INFORMATION 14
   KEY CONCEPTS 15
   KEY WORDS 31
      DO 33
      SAY 37
      BRETHREN 41
      JUDGE 45
      FAITH 49
      PERFECT 53
      PRAY 55
      LAW 59
      ENDURANCE 63
      SIN 67
      RICH 69
      WISDOM 71
   OPTIONAL WORDS 75
   KEY CONCLUSIONS 76
   MY KEY WORDS 77

THE EPISTLE OF JUDE 80
STUDYING JUDE 81
GENERAL INFORMATION 82
KEY CONCEPTS 83
KEY WORDS 92
JESUS 93
BELOVED 97
UNGODLY 99
JUDGMENT 103
ETERNAL 107
KEPT 109
MERCY 111
OPTIONAL WORDS 113
KEY CONCLUSIONS 114
MY KEY WORDS 115

BIBLE KEYWORDING GUIDE
Beyond the Highlighter

JAMES & JUDE

ROB SINCLAIR

INTRODUCTION

BEYOND THE HIGHLIGHTER

As a preacher, I am regularly asked, "I have read the Bible cover to cover several times; what do I do next?" Maybe you have asked something similar regarding your own Bible study and have felt disengaged from God's Word. My answer is to study a Bible book more in depth than you've ever thought possible...and make it look easy with the *Bible Keywording Guide*.

The *Bible Keywording Guide* (BKG) is an easy-to-use series of manuals designed to help Bible students of any level identify and mark critical information found in each book of the Bible. This includes things like: key words, purpose statements, prayers, etc. Each Bible book has its own set of peculiarities that, when marked, help the reader understand what the author is really saying.

I was told once by a friend that before he understood what keywording was, a mechanical pencil and a yellow highlighter were "standard procedure" when it came to marking important ideas and insights in his Bible. Maybe this sentiment has been true for you as well. Engage in this process and see how the *Bible Keywording Guide* will take you beyond the highlighter and bring you to a whole new level of Bible study!

THE IMPORTANCE OF KEYWORDING

WHAT IS A KEY WORD? – A key word is a word that holds a significant theological meaning and is often repeated by the author to convey his points and purposes for writing. Key words are related to the themes and overall scope of the books. Without them, the author's emphasis and meanings would be greatly diminished, and even nonexistent in many cases. Keywording is an essential component of Bible study (i.e. exegesis) and is done using colors and/or symbols to distinguish certain words in the text. Leave the highlighter in the drawer...you're using a dynamic and multicolored system now!

FREQUENCY – Some key words are used a lot; others are used less frequently. If a writer uses a word consistently – repeating it over and over – then that word is a key word. Sometimes, however, key words are used less frequently and may not be as noticeable, purely based on quantity. Words like *of* and *the* would not be considered key words, even though they are some of the most frequently used words in the Bible. On the other hand, some words are extremely theologically charged, but aren't used much. For example, *wisdom* (*sophia*) is a very important and theologically significant word in the book of James, but it is only used five times in the letter.

WORD FAMILIES – Word families are filtered in the BKG to make keywording even easier. Root words and lemmas will be distinguished in this guide with an *R* or *L*. A root word (*R*) is a word that encompasses an entire family of words joined together by the same stem, whereas a lemma (*L*) is a specific word within that root's family. This distinction is made in the BKG due to the fact that sometimes an entire family of words helps the reader understand how the writer is developing a particular concept. On the other hand, sometimes only a particular word within that larger word family is theologically significant. An excellent example to distinguish the importance of these elements would be the root word, *kaleō*, which means "to call" or "to invite." Words like *parakaleō* (*comfort/urge*), *paraklēsis* (*exhort*), and *ekklēsia* (*church/assembly*) are all lemma forms of the root word *kaleō*. If the key word to be marked is *ekklēsia*, then there is no need to mark all forms of its root word, *kaleō*.

CHAPTER-SPECIFIC KEY WORDS – Most key words in a Bible book are used throughout the entire work, but some only make a strong appearance in a chapter or two. Consider *wisdom* (*sophia*) again. Of its 28 uses in 1 Corinthians, *wisdom* appears 26 times in the first three chapters. The idea may be present in other parts of the book, but the word itself doesn't make much of an appearance elsewhere. Just because a word makes a strong showing for a few chapters, and then very little afterwards, does not mean it isn't a key word. Chapter-specific key words must still be considered because of their theological contributions to their books.

OPTIONAL WORDS – Most of these guides will contain an "Optional Words" list. Optional Words will be those words that are of some interest, but may not be used for a few different reasons: (1) they may not be exceedingly theologically significant, (2) they may be used so frequently that to mark them would mean making your Bible pages extremely crowded or too busy to focus on the other words marked, or (3) they may just be synonyms to the key words. It will be at the user's discretion whether or not to mark these words. In cases where references for these words are not provided, a Biblical concordance will help you identify their uses if you choose to mark them.

KEY CONCEPTS

The BKG will also assist you in the identification and marking of other important exegetical/Bible study elements when available. For instance, the New Testament epistles will contain things like purpose statements, prayers, and petition verbs. (Don't worry; we'll get into that later!) Many books in the Old Testament will have important textual markers and key phrases that should be marked to better understand the thought and flow of the book. With these guides, you won't miss a thing!

When available, dates of books, authors, genres, places of writing, recipients of the book, occasion of the book, etc. will be included to assist you in the study process. These elements help to form the context of each book and should be generally understood as you begin marking your Bible.

WHY YOU SHOULD KEYWORD YOUR BIBLE

SIMPLICITY – The BKG will give you a comprehensive list of all the key words in each book you're studying. You won't have to waste any time trying to determine which words and concepts you should be focusing on.

EMPHASIS ON ORIGINAL LANGUAGES – Not only will you have a complete list of key words, but you will know where those words occur in the *original language*. THIS IS THE HEART AND SOUL OF KEYWORDING! **HERE'S WHY:**

Some key words are translated differently in English while the original language never changes. A good example is the word *faith*. In many New Testament books, *faith* (*pisteuō*) is also translated as "believe," "entrusted," "sure," etc., but it remains the same Greek word. An untrained eye will miss these instances, but the BKG eliminates the possibility of overlooking or missing a key word in literal translations because of its emphasis on the original languages. Why settle for a method that only teaches you to look for certain English words when the BKG streamlines the process in the author's original language?

It's also important to realize that some words in English Bibles are not always identical in meaning. One of the best examples of this would be the word *love* in John 21:15-17. The first two times Jesus asks Peter if he loves Him, Jesus says, "Do you love (*agapaō*) Me?" to which Peter replies, "Yes, Lord; You know that I love (*phileō*) You." If the reader is not careful, he will have missed the fact that the Greek word for *love* changed a few times in this passage, thinking that the same idea for love was present for this entire encounter. The BKG will help identify these types of occurrences so that the true meaning of the text will be revealed.

NOTE: While keywording passages using this guide, you may realize that you will skip over the English word several times without marking it. Don't be alarmed! This simply means that the word, although translated in English, is not the Greek, Hebrew, or Aramaic word you are supposed to mark. Again, if you mark every occurrence of *love* the same way, you will accidentally equate *agapaō* and *phileō*. However, this should not discourage you from marking synonyms in the text if they are indeed synonyms.

FASTER AND EASIER STUDY – Once your Bible is marked, you will immediately notice the important things next time you open it to study. Do you want to study *suffering* in 1 Peter or show someone how James writes about *wisdom*? Just turn there in your marked Bible and you will see these concepts fly off the page! You won't have to spend precious time scanning paragraph after paragraph for specific words or concepts anymore. Plus, you'll notice how all of those verses are related to one another instantly!

YOUR BIBLE WILL BE BEAUTIFUL – There's something incredibly satisfying about looking down at a freshly marked page of the Bible. Not only will it give you an amazing sense of accomplishment, it could very well inspire your friends and family to study God's Word with you! Marked Bibles tend to be eye-catching and often spark interest in others.

CUSTOMIZE: MAKE YOUR MARK

COMPLETE CUSTOMIZATION – One of the many advantages of the BKG is that it allows for complete customization. Suggestions for colors and symbols will be provided throughout the guides, but you can always decide (and design) for yourself which symbol or mark you'd rather use in the "My Mark" sections. If you just hate the color orange, mix it up and develop your own color system! The suggestions given generally follow a certain pattern (i.e. red is usually used for negative things – yellow is generally used for bright things, etc.). If you don't want to mark one of the key words for whatever reason, simply leave the "Marked" box unchecked for future reference.

"MY KEY WORDS" – If you find some words during your study that you believe are key to the text but are not listed in the guide, add them to the "My Key Words" section toward the back. Fill in the information for these words and design your own symbol for them!

DO SOME COLORFUL RESEARCH – Before you begin marking your Bible, do some research and determine which markers, pens, or pencils suit *your* needs and *your* Bible the best. Some Bible pages are too thin to handle certain brands of markers, and the markers bleed through very easily. Even if a brand of markers is marketed as Bible friendly, caution and experimentation should be used prior to commitment. Feel free to use a combination of these writing utensils. I personally enjoy using colored pencils because they never bleed through, rarely fade, are cost effective, and are standardized in color within their brands.

NOTE: Make sure you have a ruler or other straight edge available when marking straight lines. Squiggly lines made by freehand can look messy!

CHOOSE YOUR LITERAL TRANSLATION

THE BKG IS COMPATIBLE WITH LITERAL TRANSLATIONS OF THE BIBLE – Scriptures in the BKG come from the *New American Standard Bible* (NASB), 1995 update. This translation was chosen for these guides because it remains one of the smoothest and yet most literal translations available on today's market. Other recommended translations to accompany this guide would be the *English Standard Version* (ESV), the *New King James Version* (NKJV), the *King James Version* (KJV), or the *Revised Standard Version* (RSV). Even though the English key words will differ in these translations on occasion (e.g. *brethren* vs. *brothers*), it is still very easy to understand which word should be keyworded to the original languages using this guide.

NOTE: Wide margin Bibles are ideal for keywording! With the amount of marking, underlining, list making, etc. it will be more convenient to have some margin space to play with.

NOTE: On extremely rare occasions it will look like a word is missing in some of the Key Word tables, having been replaced with a (●). Don't worry! This simply means that on this uncommon occasion, the translators are telling us that the original word is there, but is very cumbersome to translate and make it make sense in English given the grammar of the rest of the sentence. Mark these instances as well and know that the meaning of the verse hasn't been changed, but the insertion of the word would make the sentence too awkward in English.

PARAPHRASES AND KEYWORDING – Literal translations are essential to effective keywording. In fact, it is not possible to keyword paraphrased versions like *The Message* because they are not based on the original languages. These versions are more concerned with concepts and not the actual words of the original text.

DYNAMIC EQUIVALENCY AND KEYWORDING – It is possible to keyword translations like the *New Living Translation* (NLT) and the *New International Version* (NIV), but it is not recommended. Translations such as these were translated using the Dynamic Equivalency method, which does not highly emphasize the original languages and sacrifices literality for readability. This is seen very clearly in that the NLT and NIV sometimes translate one Greek word upwards of ten different ways in English to help the reader understand the meaning. However, the meaning actually becomes less clear with every additional word—which many times isn't even synonymous—used in place of the original word.

THE USER SHOULD NOTE that keywording the Biblical text is only one part in the study process. It is not the purpose of the BKG to identify *ALL* important elements in a text, but rather to aid in the identification of key words that may go unseen in English translations.

Certain additional facts and elements will be provided when warranted, but will not be exhaustive. Things such as places, expressions of time, lists, comparisons, contrasts, causes and effects, figures of speech, important conjunctions, verbs, pronouns, etc. will be identified at times, but not extensively since they can be identified in English. However, after the text is keyworded, finding most of these other things will be much easier.

"But prove yourselves doers of the word, and not merely hearers who delude themselves."

James 1:22

THE EPISTLE OF JAMES

STUDYING JAMES

1. Read the introduction to one of these guides at least once.
2. Read the "General Information" page to orient yourself to James' epistle.
3. Read James all the way through several times to familiarize yourself with the text.
4. Follow the directions found under "Key Concepts." This section will have you mark other important things prior to keywording the book.
5. Keyword the book:
    a. Turn to the first keywording page (e.g. *Do*) and locate the suggested symbol for that particular word.
    b. Use the reference list provided in order to locate the English words in your Bible that correspond to their respective Greek word.
    c. Mark the located word with the suggested symbol. Do this for all the key words provided in each guide.
    d. When applicable, answer the questions and/or follow the study prompts included for the words.
    e. For an even deeper study of the word, define it using a reputable Bible dictionary.
6. Mark the Optional Words at your own discretion using the suggested symbols or by creating your own.
7. Complete the "Key Conclusions" section.
8. Utilize the "My Key Words" section when applicable.

GENERAL INFORMATION

AUTHOR	JAMES The brother of Jesus (cf. Matt. 13:55; Mark 6:3)
GENRE	GENERAL EPISTLE
DATE	c. 47 A.D.
WRITTEN FR.	JERUSALEM
RECIPIENTS	TO THE TWELVE TRIBES WHO ARE DISPERSED ABROAD (1:1) Jewish Christians living outside of Palestine Not any one specific congregation
OCCASION	Since James was reputed to be a "pillar" in the early church (Gal. 2:9) and seemed to network outside of Jerusalem (Gal. 2:12), he had a good pulse on what was happening in other congregations. He wrote his letter to those in the outlying areas beyond Palestine in order to address the common problems he was hearing about. Some of these problems included: the endurance of trials, the allure of riches, controlling the tongue, and generally living life with Godly wisdom.

KEY CONCEPTS

JAMES THE LORD'S BROTHER

Like most, James had some transformation to undergo before he became a person who would advocate, let alone die, for Jesus. He went from being Jesus' unbelieving and calloused brother (John 7:1-9) to a "bond-servant of God and of the Lord Jesus Christ" (James 1:1). It must have been a curious situation being the younger brother of the Messiah, but James embraced the truth and never looked back. The chart below does not contain every shred of explicit information or implication regarding James' life, but it will give you clues as to what his journey was like and what led him to become one of the authors of the New Testament.

DATE	VERSE	EVENT
A.D. 17	1 Corinthians 9:5	James is likely married by this time – Approximately 20 years old
A.D. 26	John 2:12	Jesus' brothers, including James, are with Him at the feast in Cana.
A.D. 27	Matthew 13:55; Mark 6:3	Jesus' last visit to Nazareth – James listed as one of His brothers.
A.D. 29	John 7:1-9	Jesus' brothers, including James, still don't believe in Him.
A.D. 30	1 Corinthians 15:7	James is listed as one of the many whom the Lord Jesus appeared to after His resurrection.
A.D. 30	Acts 1:13-14	Jesus' brothers are listed as having been in the upper room after His ascension.
A.D. 37	Acts 9:26-29; Galatians 1:18-19	Paul goes to Jerusalem after his conversion and three-year hiatus in Arabia. James is listed as working with the apostles at this time.
A.D. 47	Acts 12:17	James is mentioned again as being a leader in the Jerusalem church.
A.D. 47	James 1:1	**JAMES AUTHORS HIS EPISTLE**

A.D. 49	Acts 15:13-29; Galatians 2:1-10	James addresses the Jerusalem council regarding the Gentiles and the Law. Here, he's listed as being a "pillar" of the church.
A.D. 49	Galatians 2:12	James sends a delegation to Antioch to possibly follow up the Jerusalem conference and inspect the work.
A.D. 57	Acts 21:17-26	Paul finishes his third missionary journey and comes to Jerusalem where James is still leading the Jerusalem church alongside the elders.
A.D. 62	Josephus, *Antiquities of the Jews* XX.9.1.	Josephus tells us that James was stoned to death.
A.D. 69	Jude 1	Jude notes that he and James are brothers.

Question:

📖 What events in James' life stand out to you that likely caused his change in attitude toward his brother, Jesus?

📖 How would you summarize James' work in Christ's kingdom once he became convinced of who his brother was?

Notes:

PURPOSE STATEMENT

While James never said, "I'm writing this letter because..." he does pen some powerful verses that summarize the heart of his message. Since the letter is so power-packed and others-oriented, scholars have suggested several passages as James' purpose for writing – including: 1:26-27 & 5:19-20. However, once a person realizes how James' desire for his readers to embody practical and loving Christianity permeates every page of his letter, a few other compelling verses come to mind:

"But prove yourselves doers of the word, and not merely hearers who delude themselves."	1:22
"If, however, you are fulfilling the royal law according to the Scripture, "You shall love your neighbor as yourself," you are doing well."	2:8
"So speak and so act as those who are to be judged by the law of liberty."	2:12
"Who among you is wise and understanding? Let him show by his good behavior his deeds in the gentleness of wisdom."	3:13

Suggestion: Underline these verses using a distinct color. (Orange?)

Marked: ☐   **My Mark:**

Question:

📖 Which of the suggested verses, if any, do you believe stand as the core message of James' letter? If you wish, come back to this question after keywording the book.

Notes:

IMPERATIVES

It's clear from the Scriptures that James became a very prominent figure in the Jerusalem church. He is no soft-spoken person and is often seen among the leadership as one who voices his concerns and offers his advice. Just as Peter is often thought of in connection with the church in Rome, so James is to Jerusalem. Simply put, he has the authority to tell people they need to do better. James uses no fewer than 62 imperatives in his letter to spur his readers into spiritual action and thinking. In James, an imperative will sound like: "consider it all joy" – "prove yourselves" – "so speak" – "so act" – "draw near to God" – "humble yourselves" – "be patient" – and so on. Look for these command words in James' epistle and list them in the chart below if you'd like. Be mindful of the fact that some of James' imperatives are used in illustrations and are not necessarily direct commands to the readers (e.g. 2:16 – "and one of you says to them, "***Go** in peace, **be warmed** and **be filled**,*").

CAUTION: Many of the imperatives in James are also key words to the book! Be careful that if you mark imperatives rather than list them, there could be some symbol confusion. However, if you have a clever way to mark a word as both an imperative and a key word, go for it!

My Mark - IMPERATIVES: ☐

VERSE	IMPERATIVE
1:2	"Consider it all joy"

Notes:

PARALLELS TO THE SERMON ON THE MOUNT

It shouldn't surprise us that James derives much of his teaching from his famous big brother. In many passages, James takes what Jesus said in His Sermon on the Mount in Matthew 5-7 and Luke 6 and gives another everyday application. It's almost like James is saying, "See! This real life situation is exactly what Jesus was talking about!" Since Matthew wouldn't write the words of Jesus in his gospel for another decade, James actually gives us the first written version of the Sermon on the Mount. The chart below contains many of the parallels between James' epistle and Jesus' teachings. If you find more that you'd like to add, use the blank spaces below. Due to the large volume of comparable verses, you may find it useful to simply keep this chart as a reference. If you'd like to indicate these parallels in your Bible, see the symbol suggestion below the chart.

JAMES	SERMON ON THE MOUNT	SUBJECT
1:2	Mt. 5:10-12; Lk. 6:22, 23	Consider trials with joy
1:4	Mt. 5:48	Be perfect and complete
1:5, 17	Mt. 7:7-11; Lk. 11:9	Ask God for good gifts
1:10, 11	Mt. 6:28-30	Lessons from the field
1:14, 15	Mt. 5:28	The dangers of lust
1:19, 20	Mt. 5:22	Discussion of anger
1:22, 23	Mt. 7:24-27	Hearing and doing the Word
1:26, 27	Mt. 7:21-23	Worthless religion
2:5	Mt. 5:3; Lk. 6:20	Poor as heirs of the kingdom
2:8, 10	Mt. 5:19, 20	Keep the moral/royal law
2:11	Mt. 5:21, 22	Discussion of murder
2:13	Mt. 5:7; 6:14, 15	Showing mercy
2:14-26	Mt. 7:21-23; Lk. 6:46	Dead faith
3:12	Mt. 7:16; Lk. 6:43-45	Fruit produced in its kind
3:18	Mt. 5:9	Blessed are the peacemakers
4:2, 3	Mt. 7:7, 8; Lk. 11:9, 10	Ask and receive
4:4	Mt. 6:24	Serving two masters
4:8	Mt. 5:8	Blessed are the pure in heart
4:9, 10	Mt. 5:4	Blessed are those who mourn
4:11, 12	Mt. 7:1-5; Lk. 6:37	Wrongly judging your brother

4:13, 14	Mt. 6:34	The business of tomorrow
5:1	Lk. 6:24, 25	Woe to the rich
5:2-5	Mt. 6:19-21	Moth and rust destroy earthly riches
5:9	Mt. 5:22; 7:1	Wrongly judging your brother
5:10, 11	Mt. 5:12	The prophets as examples
5:12	Mt. 5:33-37	'Yes, yes' & 'No, no'

Suggestion: Draw a symbol over the verse number in James. (e.g. 🔺)
You may also simply want to write the parallel verses of Jesus' sermon in your margin next to James' instruction.

Marked: ☐   **My Mark:**

Notes:

JEWISH NATURE OF THE LETTER

Another distinctive feature of James' epistle is that of its Jewish nature. Remember that James is writing during a time in which the church is still predominantly made up of Jewish Christians, so he uses certain Jewish buzz words that capture his readers' attention. However, it is still very likely that there were Gentiles in some of the congregations that received this letter since the Gospel had indeed reached the ears of those outside of Palestine at least a decade prior to James' writing. You may want to draw a symbol in your margin as you come to each name or term below indicating that James has made a Jewish reference (or at least a reference that Jews would understand better). See the symbol suggestion below the charts.

Note: Be careful if you choose to mark the terms themselves, rather than drawing in the margin, because the word *law* is a key word in James and has a different suggested symbol.

VERSE	TERM	MARKED
1:1	"twelve tribes"	☐
2:2	"assembly" – literally, "synagogue"	☐
2:8-12; 4:11-12	"law"	☐
2:21	"our father" (speaking of Abraham)	☐
5:4	"the Lord of Sabaoth" (cf. Rom. 9:29; Is. 1:9)	☐
5:10	"the prophets"	☐

VERSE	NAME	MARKED
2:21, 23	Abraham	☐
2:25	Rahab	☐
5:11	Job	☐
5:17	Elijah	☐

Suggestion: Draw a symbol in the margin of these verses. (✡?)

Marked: ☐   **My Mark:**

Notes:

THINK – SAY – DO

The letter of James contains a large array of topics that encompass complete Christian living. Although one might categorize James' method of instruction in different ways, it seems that his basic approach to propelling his readers into spiritual maturation and wisdom is to guide and correct them in the ways they should think, speak, and act. James gives both positive and negative direction in these areas. There are things we should think and not think – say and not say – do and not do. You may find it useful to categorize James' teachings in this way using the chart below. Keep in mind that James' instruction in these areas don't always explicitly say "do this" or "do that" – "say this" or "say that." An example of this might be "doubting" (1:6) for the "Don't Think" column.

THINK	DON'T THINK

Notes:

SAY	DON'T SAY

Notes:

DO	DON'T DO

Notes:

KEY WORDS

DO

The book of James has been deemed "The Practical Guide to Christian Living" – a fitting summary due to the sheer volume of instruction that James delivers. James emphasizes authentic Christianity by insisting that his readers not only have faith, but actually put that belief into practice by *doing*, *acting*, *behaving*, and *working* to that effect. Christianity is not meant to be a secret society of people who know certain things that others do not, but a group of sanctified people who *work* in their Lord's kingdom to encourage one another and influence the lost to seek the Lord. What hope do we have to do this if we simply claim to believe, but produce nothing in practicality? "What use is it my brethren, if someone says he has faith, but he has no works? Can that faith save him?" (2:14).

WORD	GREEK-R	TRANSLITERATION	OCCURRENCES	SUGGESTED SYMBOL
Do	ποιεω	poieō	17	Do (shovel)

Marked: ☐   **My Mark:**

James 1:22	But prove yourselves	doers	of the word, and not merely
James 1:23	is a hearer of the word and not a	doer	, he is like a man who looks at
James 1:25	forgetful hearer but an effectual	doer	, this man will be blessed in what
James 1:25	man will be blessed in what he	does	.
James 2:8	neighbor as yourself," you are	doing	well.
James 2:12	So speak and so	act	as those who are to be judged by
James 2:13	*will be* merciless to one who has	shown	no mercy; mercy triumphs over
James 2:19	You believe that God is one. You	do	well; the demons also believe, and
James 3:12	Can a fig tree, my brethren,	produce	olives, or a vine produce figs?
James 3:12	produce figs? Nor *can* salt water	produce	fresh.
James 3:18	is sown in peace by those who	make	peace.
James 4:11	you judge the law, you are not a	doer	of the law but a judge *of it*.
James 4:13	go to such and such a city, and	spend	a year there and engage in
James 4:15	Lord wills, we will live and also	do	this or that."
James 4:17	one who knows *the* right thing to	do	and does not do it, to him it is
James 4:17	right thing to do and does not	do	it, to him it is sin.
James 5:15	will raise him up, and if he has	committed	sins, they will be forgiven him.

WORD	GREEK-R	TRANSLITERATION	OCCURRENCES	SUGGESTED SYMBOL
Work	εργον	*ergon*	21	Work

Marked: ☐ **My Mark:**

James 1:3	that the testing of your faith	produces	endurance.
James 1:4	let endurance have *its* perfect	result	, so that you may be perfect and
James 1:20	for the anger of man does not	achieve	the righteousness of God.
James 1:25	become a forgetful hearer but an	effectual	doer, this man will be blessed in
James 2:9	if you show partiality, you are	committing	sin *and* are convicted by the law
James 2:14	says he has faith but he has no	works	? Can that faith save him?
James 2:17	Even so faith, if it has no	works	, is dead, *being* by itself.
James 2:18	say, "You have faith and I have	works	; show me your faith without the
James 2:18	show me your faith without the	works	, and I will show you my faith by
James 2:18	I will show you my faith by my	works	."
James 2:20	fellow, that faith without	works	is useless?
James 2:21	Abraham our father justified by	works	when he offered up Isaac his son
James 2:22	You see that faith was	working	with his works, and as a result of
James 2:22	that faith was working with his	works	, and as a result of the works,
James 2:22	his works, and as a result of the	works	, faith was perfected;
James 2:24	see that a man is justified by	works	and not by faith alone.
James 2:25	the harlot also justified by	works	when she received the messengers
James 2:26	is dead, so also faith without	works	is dead.
James 3:13	show by his good behavior his	deeds	in the gentleness of wisdom.
James 5:4	Behold, the pay of the	laborers	who mowed your fields, *and* which
James 5:16	so that you may be healed. The	effective	prayer of a righteous man can

WORD	GREEK-L	TRANSLITERATION	OCC...	SUGGESTED SYMBOL
Behavior	ἀναστροφή	*anastrophē*	1	Behavior

Marked: ☐   **My Mark:**

James 3:13	Let him show by his good	behavior	his deeds in the gentleness of

Study:

🔍 As you study and keyword the *doing* terms in James as part of this section, pair your observations with those you made in the "Think-Say-Do" section under "Key Concepts."

🔍 Look these *doing* words up in your Bible dictionary and compare their definitions.

Definition of *poieō*:

Definition of *ergon*:

Definition of *anastrophē*:

Question:

📖 What do you suppose it means to be a ***doer of the word***? (cf. 1:22-25)

📖 What are some practical situations James applies these terms to?

📖 Would you consider yourself a *doer* of the word? Why or why not?

Notes:

SAY

Christian behavior is not only embodied in what a person does, but also in what a person *says*. It doesn't matter if people perform great acts of kindness or wonderful works for the Lord if their words are a constant undoing. Anger, pride, and cursing are just a few foibles of the tongue that James discusses. One word spoken wrongly and sinfully can undo much good and ruin even the best of reputations. James says that the tongue is a fire, and cautions us to "See how great a forest is set aflame by such a small fire!" (3:5). As you mark the *mouth* words, notice how important it is to James that his readers use their words wisely. Ultimately, the Lord's brother cautions everyone to "So *speak* and so act as those who are to be judged by the law of liberty" (2:12).

WORD	GREEK-R	TRANSLITERATION	OCCURRENCES	SUGGESTED SYMBOL
Say	λεγω	legō	24	◁Say◉

Marked: ☐   **My Mark:**

James 1:13	Let no one	say	when he is tempted, "I am being
James 1:18	will He brought us forth by the	word	of truth, so that we would be a
James 1:21	in humility receive the	word	implanted, which is able to save
James 1:22	prove yourselves doers of the	word	, and not merely hearers who
James 1:22	and not merely hearers who	delude	themselves.
James 1:23	For if anyone is a hearer of the	word	and not a doer, he is like a man
James 2:3	is wearing the fine clothes, and	say	, "You sit here in a good place,"
James 2:3	here in a good place," and you	say	to the poor man, "You stand over
James 2:4	and become judges with evil	motives	?
James 2:5	beloved brethren: did not God	choose	the poor of this world *to be* rich
James 2:11	For He who	said	, "DO NOT COMMIT ADULTERY," also
James 2:11	DO NOT COMMIT ADULTERY," also	said	, "DO NOT COMMIT MURDER." Now if
James 2:14	is it, my brethren, if someone	says	he has faith but he has no works?
James 2:16	and one of you	says	to them, "Go in peace, be warmed
James 2:18	But someone may *well*	say	, "You have faith and I have
James 2:23	the Scripture was fulfilled which	says	, "AND ABRAHAM BELIEVED GOD,

James 2:23	AND IT WAS	RECKONED	TO HIM AS RIGHTEOUSNESS," and he
James 3:2	does not stumble in what he	says	, he is a perfect man, able to
James 3:9	With it we	bless	our Lord and Father, and with it
James 3:10	from the same mouth come *both*	blessing	and cursing. My brethren, these
James 4:5	do you think that the Scripture	speaks	to no purpose: "He jealously
James 4:6	a greater grace. Therefore *it*	says	, "GOD IS OPPOSED TO THE PROUD,
James 4:13	Come now, you who	say	, "Today or tomorrow we will go to
James 4:15	Instead, *you ought* to	say	, "If the Lord wills, we will live

WORD	GREEK-R	TRANSLITERATION	OCCURRENCES	SUGGESTED SYMBOL
Speak	λαλεω	*laleō*	6	◁Speak◉

Marked: ☐   **My Mark:**

James 1:19	must be quick to hear, slow to	speak	*and* slow to anger;
James 2:12	So	speak	and so act as those who are to be
James 4:11	Do not	speak	against one another, brethren. He
James 4:11	one another, brethren. He who	speaks	against a brother or judges his
James 4:11	a brother or judges his brother,	speaks	against the law and judges the
James 5:10	patience, take the prophets who	spoke	in the name of the Lord.

WORD	GREEK-R	TRANSLITERATION	OCCURRENCES	SUGGESTED SYMBOL
Tongue	γλωσσα	*glōssa*	5	Tongue

Marked: ☐   **My Mark:**

James 1:26	and yet does not bridle his	tongue	but deceives his *own* heart, this
James 3:5	So also the	tongue	is a small part of the body, and
James 3:6	And the	tongue	is a fire, the *very* world of
James 3:6	the *very* world of iniquity; the	tongue	is set among our members as that
James 3:8	But no one can tame the	tongue	; *it is* a restless evil *and* full

Study:

🔍 As you study and keyword the *speaking* terms in James as part of this section, pair your observations with those you made in the "Think-Say-Do" section under "Key Concepts."

🔍 If you'd like, locate and mark other speaking terms in James' letter with one of the suggested symbols above. What other terms relate to speech in James' letter?

Examples: *mouth (stoma)* in 3:3, 10 – *curse (katara)* in 3:9, 10 – *swear (omnyō)* in 5:12

Marked: ☐   **My Mark:**

Question:

📖 James says, "And the tongue is a fire, the very world of iniquity; the tongue is set among our members as that which defiles the entire body, and sets on fire the course of our life, and is set on fire by hell" (3:6).

How does fire illustrate what the tongue does?

How do you suppose the tongue can set the course of our lives on fire?

📖 How else does James describe the tongue?

📖 It is no coincidence that James has much to say about the tongue in Chapter 3 after having broached the subject of teachers in 3:1. Why do you suppose teachers will "incur a stricter judgment"?

📖 Which instructions regarding a person's speech stand out to you the most? Are there any scenarios James addresses that you need to work on concerning the way you use *your* words?

Notes:

BRETHREN

One cannot help but see just how much James loves the people he is writing to through his use of *brethren*, *one another*, and *love*. It is impossible to separate these words from the letter since they are the motivating forces. Why does James instruct his brethren so much? Why does he insist they act righteously? Why does he care what they say and how they say it? Because he loves them! Because he wants them to love each other and their God more every day! He says in 2:8, "If, however, you are fulfilling the royal law according to the Scripture, "You shall love your neighbor as yourself," you are doing well." Practicing love and sacrificing our own needs for those of others is deeper than well wishes. It's hard at times. It's uncomfortable. But it is what's required to be practical people of God in this lost and floundering world.

WORD	GREEK-R	TRANSLITERATION	OCCURRENCES	SUGGESTED SYMBOL
Brethren	αδελφος	*adelphos*	20	Bre♡ren

Marked: ☐ **My Mark:**

James 1:2	Consider it all joy, my	brethren	, when you encounter various
James 1:9	But the	brother	of humble circumstances is to
James 1:16	Do not be deceived, my beloved	brethren	.
James 1:19	*This* you know, my beloved	brethren	. But everyone must be quick to
James 2:1	My	brethren	, do not hold your faith in our
James 2:5	Listen, my beloved	brethren	: did not God choose the
James 2:14	What use is it, my	brethren	, if someone says he has faith but
James 2:15	If a	brother	or sister is without clothing and
James 2:15	If a brother or	sister	is without clothing and in need of
James 3:1	*of you* become teachers, my	brethren	, knowing that as such we will
James 3:10	*both* blessing and cursing. My	brethren	, these things ought not to be
James 3:12	Can a fig tree, my	brethren	, produce olives, or a vine
James 4:11	not speak against one another,	brethren	. He who speaks against a brother
James 4:11	He who speaks against a	brother	or judges his brother, speaks
James 4:11	against a brother or judges his	brother	, speaks against the law and

James 5:7	Therefore be patient,	brethren	, until the coming of the Lord.
James 5:9	Do not complain,	brethren	, against one another, so that you
James 5:10	As an example,	brethren	, of suffering and patience, take
James 5:12	But above all, my	brethren	, do not swear, either by heaven
James 5:19	My	brethren	, if any among you strays from the

WORD	GREEK-R	TRANSLITERATION	OCCURRENCES	SUGGESTED SYMBOL
Love	αγαπαω	agapaō	6	L♥ve

Marked: ☐   My Mark:

James 1:12	Lord has promised to those who	love	Him.
James 1:16	Do not be deceived, my	beloved	brethren.
James 1:19	This you know, my	beloved	brethren. But everyone must be
James 2:5	Listen, my	beloved	brethren: did not God choose the
James 2:5	which He promised to those who	love	Him?
James 2:8	to the Scripture, "YOU SHALL	LOVE	YOUR NEIGHBOR AS YOURSELF," you

WORD	GREEK-L	TRANSLITERATION	OCC...	SUGGESTED SYMBOL
One another	ἀλλήλων	allēlōn	4	One ⭕ another

Marked: ☐   My Mark:

James 4:11	Do not speak against	one another	, brethren. He who speaks
James 5:9	brethren, against	one another	, so that you yourselves
James 5:16	confess your sins to	one another	, and pray for one another
James 5:16	and pray for	one another	so that you may be healed.

Study:

🔍 While James makes a tremendous effort to get his readers to examine themselves and correct their shortcomings, his underlying goal is that they would look beyond themselves and look after the interests of others. As stated earlier, this plea by James is clearest in his call for them to fulfill the royal law (2:8). *Law* is also a key word in James, so the royal law will be discussed further in that section.

Question:

📖 Based on his instructions regarding *one another*, what do you think were some of the problems facing James' readers?

📖 In light of his instructions in 2:14-26, why do you think James consistently calls his readers *brethren* and reinforces the concepts of *love* and *one another*?

📖 What lessons for your own life do you see in James' instructions regarding *brethren*, *love*, and *one another*?

Notes:

JUDGE

James undoubtedly reflects His big brother's teachings regarding judgment. Jesus was very straightforward in His cautions of wrongly judging others and incurring the judgment of the Father (Mt. 7:1-5; Lk. 6:37). Improper judgment of others must be checked, for it certainly affects the way we treat others and how we think and speak about them. One of the first things you will notice as you approach *judge* (*krinō*) is that it is not just a word about *doing*, but also *thinking*. Doubting, distinctions, and hypocrisy are just a few *judging* terms that have to do with the mind.

WORD	GREEK-R	TRANSLITERATION	OCCURRENCES	SUGGESTED SYMBOL
Judge	κρινω	*krinō*	20	Judge

Marked: ☐ **My Mark:**

James 1:6	he must ask in faith without any	doubting	, for the one who doubts is like
James 1:6	any doubting, for the one who	doubts	is like the surf of the sea,
James 2:4	have you not made	distinctions	among yourselves, and
James 2:4	among yourselves, and become	judges	with evil motives?
James 2:6	you and personally drag you into	court	?
James 2:12	and so act as those who are to be	judged	by *the* law of liberty.
James 2:13	For	judgment	*will be* merciless to one who has
James 2:13	no mercy; mercy triumphs over	judgment	.
James 3:1	as such we will incur a stricter	judgment	.
James 3:17	full of mercy and good fruits,	unwavering	, without hypocrisy.
James 3:17	good fruits, unwavering, without	hypocrisy	.
James 4:11	who speaks against a brother or	judges	his brother, speaks against the
James 4:11	speaks against the law and	judges	the law; but if you judge the law,
James 4:11	and judges the law; but if you	judge	the law, you are not a doer of the
James 4:11	are not a doer of the law but a	judge	of it.
James 4:12	There is *only* one Lawgiver and	Judge	, the One who is able to save and
James 4:12	to destroy; but who are you who	judge	your neighbor?

James 5:9	so that you yourselves may not be	judged	; behold, the Judge is standing
James 5:9	may not be judged; behold, the	Judge	is standing right at the door.
James 5:12	so that you may not fall under	judgment	.

Study:

🔍 Notice again that it is the royal law (law of liberty) that will *judge* how we treat and speak of our neighbors (2:12). Keep following James' instructions surrounding this law as we approach *law* as a key word in a few pages. What is your understanding of this law so far? (cf. 1:25; 2:8, 12)

🔍 You may also want to mark *personal favoritism* (2:1), *special attention* (2:3), and *partiality* (2:9) with a similar symbol.

Marked: ☐   **My Mark:**

Question:

📖 Doubting, distinctions, and hypocrisy are some of the more unique lemma forms of *krinō*. How would you characterize these terms as *judging* words?

📖 Have you ever been guilty of showing partiality to one person over another? Why is this easy to do sometimes? What does James suggest to overcome this attitude?

📖 What other things does James say will cause us to be *judged*?

📖 What seems to be James' main point in his discussions on *judgment*?

Notes:

FAITH

To define *faith* as simply believing in something is an injustice. The Christian faith stands as that element in a person's life that he or she can choose to gain or lose – demonstrate or conceal – use or squander. James implores his readers to consider their lives of faith. He knows that they are experiencing trials and that even the most mature Christian's faith can wane in the face of temptation and adversity. Is God even listening? Does God even care how my life is lived? James spurs these believers on, persuading them to endure – to help each other – to prove themselves doers of the word – to talk to God – to know that He is listening and cares for them.

WORD	GREEK-R	TRANSLITERATION	OCCURRENCES	SUGGESTED SYMBOL
Faith	πιστευω	*pisteuō*	19	Faith

Marked: ☐   **My Mark:**

James 1:3	knowing that the testing of your	faith	produces endurance.
James 1:6	But he must ask in	faith	without any doubting, for the one
James 2:1	My brethren, do not hold your	faith	in our glorious Lord Jesus Christ
James 2:5	poor of this world *to be* rich in	faith	and heirs of the kingdom which He
James 2:14	brethren, if someone says he has	faith	but he has no works? Can that
James 2:14	but he has no works? Can that	faith	save him?
James 2:17	Even so	faith	, if it has no works, is dead,
James 2:18	someone may *well* say, "You have	faith	and I have works; show me your
James 2:18	and I have works; show me your	faith	without the works, and I will show
James 2:18	the works, and I will show you my	faith	by my works."
James 2:19	You	believe	that God is one. You do well; the
James 2:19	one. You do well; the demons also	believe	, and shudder.
James 2:20	you foolish fellow, that	faith	without works is useless?
James 2:22	You see that	faith	was working with his works, and as
James 2:22	and as a result of the works,	faith	was perfected;
James 2:23	which says, "AND ABRAHAM	BELIEVED	GOD, AND IT WAS RECKONED TO HIM
James 2:24	is justified by works and not by	faith	alone.

| James 2:26 | the spirit is dead, so also | faith | without works is dead. |
| James 5:15 | and the prayer offered in | faith | will restore the one who is sick, |

Question:

📖 James says, "Consider it all joy, my brethren, when you encounter various trials, knowing that the testing of your *faith* produces endurance." How would you summarize the concept of *faith* being tested? Do trials cause people to give up their beliefs that easily? What does James mean here?

📖 According to James Chapter 2, when is *faith* useless and dead?

📖 What can we learn from the faith of demons in 2:19? Is believing in God enough to be saved? What does a believing demon lack?

📖 According to James, how is *faith* perfected (or completed) by works? How do the examples of Abraham (2:21-24) and Rahab (2:25) help you understand this concept? What if they believed God, but never did anything about it?

📖 Who do you know personally that exemplifies this type of *faith*?

📖 Do you embody the working *faith* that James is talking about? Why or why not?

Notes:

PERFECT

When we hear the word *perfect*, we tend to think in terms of being flawless. However, the word that James uses is *teleios* (lemma form of *telos*), which means "complete" or "mature." James wants these Christians to grow. His desire is for them to be well-rounded with nothing missing in their spiritual walks. If they do the right things, but have the wrong motives and mindset, they are not *perfect*. The same goes for saying the right words to people, like "be warmed and be filled," but not acting accordingly by giving them what is necessary for the body (2:16). Our situation is no different. Believing that we are complete, mature Christians by doing well in one area of our spirituality is a delusion. We cannot rest on our laurels of earthly achievement and coast into our reward!

WORD	GREEK-R	TRANSLITERATION	OCCURRENCES	SUGGESTED SYMBOL
Perfect	τελος	*telos*	9	Perfect

Marked: ☐   **My Mark:**

James 1:4	And let endurance have *its*	perfect	result, so that you may be perfect
James 1:4	result, so that you may be	perfect	and complete, lacking in nothing.
James 1:15	birth to sin; and when sin is	accomplished	, it brings forth death.
James 1:17	good thing given and every	perfect	gift is from above, coming down
James 1:25	one who looks intently at the	perfect	law, the *law* of liberty, and
James 2:8	If, however, you are	fulfilling	the royal law according to the
James 2:22	a result of the works, faith was	perfected	;
James 3:2	stumble in what he says, he is a	perfect	man, able to bridle the whole body
James 5:11	of Job and have seen the	outcome	of the Lord's dealings, that the

WORD	GREEK-R	TRANSLITERATION	OCCURRENCES	SUGGESTED SYMBOL
Complete	ολος	*olos*	5	Complete

Marked: ☐   **My Mark:**

James 1:4	so that you may be perfect and	complete	, lacking in nothing.

James 2:10	For whoever keeps the	whole	law and yet stumbles in one *point*,
James 3:2	able to bridle the	whole	body as well.
James 3:3	will obey us, we direct their	entire	body as well.
James 3:6	as that which defiles the	entire	body, and sets on fire the course

Study:

🔍 Define *teleios* in your Bible dictionary. What other helpful or interesting aspects are seen in its definition?

Definition of *teleios*:

Question:

📖 James tells us that it's possible through God for us to be "perfect and complete, lacking in nothing" (1:4). How would you describe the journey people must take from being incomplete (immature or imperfect) to being *perfect* in the way James discusses?

📖 What are some areas in your own life that you need to work on to reach James' description of *perfect*? Is it the way you handle trials? The way you say things? The way you think of people?

Notes:

PRAY

Have you ever prayed to God just to get something from Him? Have you ever asked Him to help you with something, but doubted that He would actually do anything? These are just a few attitudes that James tries to correct in his readers' conversations with the Almighty. James wants these Christians to approach God in prayer, for he knows that "The effective prayer of a righteous man can accomplish much" (5:16) and that the Father does in fact want to give us good things (1:5). However, prayer is more than handing God a wish list. We must also pray for those spiritual blessings, like wisdom (1:5), which help us more in this life than those fancy new material blessings we've had our eyes on. It requires maturity to understand that prayer is a cornerstone in the faithful Christian's walk. It takes discipline. It takes mindfulness. A Christian that gives up on prayer, or attempts to use it for selfish gain, puts his relationship with God in unnecessary jeopardy.

WORD	GREEK-R	TRANSLITERATION	OCCURRENCES	SUGGESTED SYMBOL
Pray	ευχομαι	*euchomai*	7	Pray

Marked: ☐   My Mark:

James 5:13	suffering? *Then* he must	pray	. Is anyone cheerful? He is to
James 5:14	of the church and they are to	pray	over him, anointing him with oil
James 5:15	and the	prayer	offered in faith will restore the
James 5:16	your sins to one another, and	pray	for one another so that you may be
James 5:17	with a nature like ours, and he	prayed	earnestly that it would not rain, and
James 5:17	a nature like ours, and he prayed	earnestly	that it would not rain, and it did
James 5:18	Then he	prayed	again, and the sky poured rain and

WORD	GREEK-R	TRANSLITERATION	OCCURRENCES	SUGGESTED SYMBOL
Ask	αιτεω	*aiteō*	5	Ask

Marked: ☐   My Mark:

James 1:5	any of you lacks wisdom, let him	ask	of God, who gives to all

James 1:6		But he must	ask	in faith without any doubting, for
James 4:2	do not have because you do not		ask	.
James 4:3		You	ask	and do not receive, because you
James 4:3	and do not receive, because you		ask	with wrong motives, so that you

WORD	GREEK-R	TRANSLITERATION	OCCURRENCES	SUGGESTED SYMBOL
Prayer	δεομαι	deomai	1	Prayer

Marked: ☐   My Mark:

James 5:16	you may be healed. The effective	prayer	of a righteous man can accomplish

Study:

- 🔍 You probably noticed that you marked both *prayed* and *earnestly* in 5:17. This is not a mistake, as both words are "praying words" that amplify one another. This verse has also been translated as, "he prayed with prayer" – "he prayed intensely" – "he prayed fervently" – etc.

- 🔍 It's not surprising that *gives* (*didōmi*) is a word that occurs in the context of *praying* to God. There are many reasons to pray to God, and asking Him to *give* us something is certainly among our motives. You may want to locate and mark *gives* in James' letter to see how our Creator responds when we come to Him in faith. (See "Optional Words" for a symbol suggestion.)

    Gives (*didōmi*): 1:5 (2x); 1:17 (*given* & *gift*); 2:16; 4:6 (2x); 5:18 (*poured*)

    Marked: ☐   My Mark:

Question:

- 📖 What problems were James' readers having with *prayer*? What does this tell us about what we should be *praying* for?

📖 What if we *pray* for something that is not God's will for our lives? Will He give me _____ just because I want it? Why or why not?

📖 In what circumstances does James say we should *pray*? How often does this suggest we should be *praying*?

📖 James tells us that Elijah "prayed earnestly" (5:17) and that the "*effective* prayer of a righteous man can accomplish much" (5:16). How would you summarize what this kind of *praying* looks like?

📖 Do you believe that *your* prayers can also influence God and accomplish much? Why or why not?

📖 What have you been praying for recently?

Notes:

LAW

It is beyond question that the term *law* is largely discussed throughout the New Testament, having reference to the Old Covenant, or the Law of Moses. While James does argue a point from the Old Law (2:8-12), the conceptual thrust of *law* in his epistle is that of the "royal law," or "law of liberty" (1:25; 2:8, 12). James is writing to former Jews who have a working knowledge of the dos and don'ts of the Law of Moses, but they must now understand *law* in relationship to Jesus Christ, the King. Note that the royal law is stated clearly in 2:8 as, "You shall love your neighbor as yourself." Although this law was given in Moses' day (Leviticus 19:18), it now governs Christians on a deeper level and with a higher standard of love than mankind has ever been called to before.

WORD	GREEK-R	TRANSLITERATION	OCCURRENCES	SUGGESTED SYMBOL
Law	νομος	*nomos*	12	Law

Marked: ☐   **My Mark:**

James 1:25	who looks intently at the perfect	law	, the *law* of liberty, and abides
James 2:5	world *to be* rich in faith and	heirs	of the kingdom which He promised
James 2:8	you are fulfilling the royal	law	according to the Scripture,
James 2:9	sin *and* are convicted by the	law	as transgressors.
James 2:10	For whoever keeps the whole	law	and yet stumbles in one *point*, he
James 2:11	have become a transgressor of the	law	.
James 2:12	those who are to be judged by *the*	law	of liberty.
James 4:11	his brother, speaks against the	law	and judges the law; but if you
James 4:11	against the law and judges the	law	; but if you judge the law, you
James 4:11	the law; but if you judge the	law	, you are not a doer of the law
James 4:11	law, you are not a doer of the	law	but a judge *of it*.
James 4:12	There is *only* one	Lawgiver	and Judge, the One who is able to

Study:

- Be sure to mark the second use of *law* in 1:25.

- Jesus is famous for many things, among which is the fact that He constantly upped the spiritual ante of the Old Law to a deeper level in the New Covenant. Review Jesus' teachings in the Sermon on the Mount in Matthew 5:21-22 & 27-28 and compare them to that of James 2:8-12 to see an example of how He does this. Keep this thought in mind as you continue to conceptualize the *Royal Law* in the next section.

- **The Royal Law:**

    In Leviticus 19:15 & 18, the concepts of "judging your neighbor fairly" and "loving your neighbor as yourself" were introduced to God's people through Moses as tangible, written laws. And just like His heightened standards for murder and adultery (see above), Jesus upsets the status quo again by making sure mankind knows that neighbors are not limited to people in your own nationality. Read Luke 10:25-37 and watch how Jesus brings a lawyer to this understanding in the parable of the Good Samaritan.

    In light of passages like Matthew 22:34-40 and Mark 12:28-34, why do you suppose James labels the law, "You shall love your neighbor as yourself" as the *Royal Law*?

    What is it about the *Royal Law* that makes it a law?

    In light of your observations and answers to the questions above, how would you now summarize the scope of the *Royal Law*? How does James get his readers to understand what it is and how to apply it?

Question:

📖 What are some practical ways that we, as Christians, can fulfill the *Royal Law*?

📖 How do we sometimes attempt to be the lawgivers where our brothers and sisters in Christ are concerned? (cf. James 4:11-12)

Notes:

ENDURANCE

If there is one thing that being human can promise us, it's that trials, temptations, and sufferings will eventually find us. This is not horrible news, however, since God has had the perfect solution to these problems in mind since the beginning of creation. He tells us through James that we can and should view our trials differently! People who belong to the world and call it their friend will think like the world (4:4) – but Christians think like Jesus! Christians understand that trials and tests of faith have the potential to bring about endurance (1:2-4). And it's this *endurance* that James tells his readers will result in being made "perfect and complete, lacking in nothing" (1:4). In the midst of a trying and antagonistic environment, James assures these Christians that the hard knocks of life are what shape and prove our character before God.

WORD	GREEK-R	TRANSLITERATION	OCCURRENCES	SUGGESTED SYMBOL
Endurance	μενω	*menō*	6	<Endurance>

Marked: ☐   **My Mark:**

James 1:3	testing of your faith produces	endurance	.
James 1:4	And let	endurance	have *its* perfect result, so that
James 1:12	Blessed is a man who	perseveres	under trial; for once he has been
James 1:25	law, the *law* of liberty, and	abides	by it, not having become a
James 5:11	We count those blessed who	endured	. You have heard of the endurance
James 5:11	endured. You have heard of the	endurance	of Job and have seen the outcome

WORD	GREEK-R	TRANSLITERATION	OCC...	SUGGESTED SYMBOL
Patience	μακροθυμεω	*makrothymeō*	4	<Patience>

Marked: ☐   **My Mark:**

James 5:7	Therefore be	patient	, brethren, until the coming of
James 5:7	produce of the soil, being	patient	about it, until it gets
James 5:8	You too be	patient	; strengthen your hearts, for the
James 5:10	brethren, of suffering and	patience	, take the prophets who spoke in

Study:

🔍 Define *hypomonē* (the primary lemma form of *menō* in James) and *makrothymeō*. How do these definitions give color to the points James makes about *patience* and *endurance*?

Definition of *hypomonē*:

_____
_____
_____

Definition of *makrothymeō*:

_____
_____
_____

🔍 As you read James, you may come across other words that also carry an element of *enduring* or being *patient*. If you'd like, mark these synonyms with a similar symbol.

Examples: *testing (dokimion)* in 1:3 – *waits (ekdechomai)* in 5:7

_____
_____

Marked: ☐ | **My Mark:**

🔍 James discusses several scenarios that have the potential to *tempt* his readers or cause them to lose their faith in the midst of *trials*. The first chapter sets the tone for these discussions, as *tempted* and *trials (peira)* occur seven times. Mark these words if you'd like. (See "Optional Words" for a symbol suggestion.)

Tempted / Trials (peira): 1:2, 12, 13 (4x), 14

Marked: ☐ | **My Mark:**

Question:

📖 Job and the prophets are mentioned as having *patience* and *endurance* (5:10-11). Without reading all 42 chapters of the book of Job, what do you remember about Job's story? What situations did he encounter that required his ultimate trust in God?

_____
_____
_____
_____

📖 Which other people from the Scriptures can you think of that were able to remain steadfast in the face of adversity? Who are your favorites? What else do they teach you about enduring trials?

📖 According to James, what are some circumstances we should expect in our own lives that will require *endurance*? Do you relate to any of the circumstances James' readers are facing?

📖 What is the result of enduring and keeping our faith through the trials of life? (cf. 1:4, 12, 25; 4:7-10, etc.)

📖 What situations are requiring *your* endurance and patience right now?

Notes:

SIN

James knows that opportunities for *sin* abound in the lives of people who seem to have the deck stacked against them. Remember that the Christians James writes to are former Jews who have been "dispersed abroad" (1:1) and are likely the extreme minority in their communities. Having transitioned from Judaism to Christianity, they probably didn't receive encouragement from their Jewish neighbors either. Living in such spiritually isolated circumstances and being surrounded by unbelieving people on a daily basis can make the ways of the world start to look a little better. As you continue to read James' letter, watch for the particular circumstances that he says are causing them to drift into *sinful* habits and mindsets.

WORD	GREEK-R	TRANSLITERATION	OCCURRENCES	SUGGESTED SYMBOL
Sin	αμαρτανω	*hamartanō*	9	(Sin)

Marked: ☐   My Mark:

James 1:15	has conceived, it gives birth to	sin	; and when sin is accomplished, it
James 1:15	it gives birth to sin; and when	sin	is accomplished, it brings forth
James 2:9	partiality, you are committing	sin	and are convicted by the law as
James 4:8	to you. Cleanse your hands, you	sinners	; and purify your hearts, you
James 4:17	and does not do it, to him it is	sin	.
James 5:15	him up, and if he has committed	sins	, they will be forgiven him.
James 5:16	Therefore, confess your	sins	to one another, and pray for one
James 5:20	let him know that he who turns a	sinner	from the error of his way will
James 5:20	and will cover a multitude of	sins	.

Study:

🔍 God is interested in saving souls, so that is the business James is about. Sin is sin, and it's called as such. James is not about to water down the Word of God "which is able to save your souls" (1:21). *Sin* has many synonyms in this letter and James pulls no punches in his vocabulary. If you'd like, look for and mark other words that indicate sinful behavior with a similar symbol.

Examples: *filthiness (rhyparia)* & *wickedness (kakia)* in 1:21 – *iniquity (adikia)* in 3:6

Marked: ☐   My Mark:

🔍 Ringing in as the opposite of *sin*, James presents *righteousness* before God as the target. If you'd like, mark these references as well. (See "Optional Words" for a symbol suggestion.)

Righteousness (dikē): 1:20; 2:23; 3:18; 5:6, 16 → Translated as *justified* in 2:21, 24, 25

Marked: ☐   My Mark:

Question:

📖 What *sinful* circumstances seem to be troubling James' readers the most?

📖 According to James, it is possible to *sin* by not doing the right thing we know we should do (4:17). Have you ever been guilty of *sin* by *not* doing something you should? When?

Notes:

RICH

Even though the word for *rich* (*ploutos*) only occurs six times in the letter, James addresses the concept in a number of ways. Being a monetarily poor Christian (1:9), being a rich Christian (1:10), interacting with the rich and poor alike (2:1-13), suffering at the hands of the rich (2:6-7), withholding necessities from fellow Christians in need (2:15-16), losing sight of God in the pursuit of riches (4:13-17), and abusing others by withholding pay (5:1-6) are just some of the money scenarios that James' readers are wrapped up in. Every one of these situations has its own set of difficulties – yes, even being rich ourselves! – and each requires *wisdom* so as to *do* the right thing, demonstrate our *faith*, and be found *perfect* and *complete* by our Creator.

WORD	GREEK-R	TRANSLITERATION	OCCURRENCES	SUGGESTED SYMBOL
Rich	πλουτος	*ploutos*	6	R$ch

Marked: ☐   **My Mark:**

James 1:10	and the	rich	man *is to glory* in his
James 1:11	is destroyed; so too the	rich	man in the midst of his pursuits
James 2:5	the poor of this world *to be*	rich	in faith and heirs of the kingdom
James 2:6	the poor man. Is it not the	rich	who oppress you and personally
James 5:1	Come now, you	rich	, weep and howl for your miseries
James 5:2	Your	riches	have rotted and your garments have

Study:

🔍 Like other key words in James, the word *rich* has a few synonyms throughout the letter. Refer back to the passages listed in the summary paragraph above and review the contexts of each. What other "money words" does James use in his discussions of *riches*?

Examples: *gold ring* & *fine clothes* (2:2) – *profit* (4:13) – *gold, silver, treasure* (5:3) – *fields* (5:4) – *luxuriously* (5:5) – etc.

Marked: ☐   **My Mark:**

Question:

📖 James 1:9 says, "But the brother of humble circumstances is to glory in his high position." Based on James' teachings on matters of perspective, what "high position" do you think he's talking about? (cf. 2:5-6; Matthew 5:3; Luke 6:20)

📖 How can having *riches* in this life be a trial for a Christian?

📖 How are you handling the physical blessings God has given you?

📖 Out of all the circumstances concerning money in James' epistle, which ones do you struggle with the most? Which ones do you fear you will not handle correctly when or if the time comes?

Notes:

WISDOM

Pick any concept in the book of James, or any area of life for that matter. Guess what? It requires *wisdom*! If we want to be people who are able to *act* appropriately, control our *speech*, monitor our *minds*, *judge* people and situations correctly, demonstrate God-fearing *faith*, love our neighbors as ourselves, *endure* trials of life, avoid *sin*, handle *riches* accordingly, and ultimately mature into *complete* Christians, we have to be *wise*. James tells his readers to ask God for *wisdom* from above (1:5). Once they gain this *wisdom*, they'll see things the way God sees them. They'll see people, money, trials, etc. the way God sees them. And *wisdom* isn't just knowing about these things, but approaching them in a righteous and practical way that shows God that we are His people who want to do things His way – because let's face it...His way is better.

WORD	GREEK-R	TRANSLITERATION	OCCURRENCES	SUGGESTED SYMBOL
Wisdom	σοφος	*sophos*	5	Wisdom

Marked: ☐   **My Mark:**

James 1:5	But if any of you lacks	wisdom	, let him ask of God, who gives to
James 3:13	Who among you is	wise	and understanding? Let him show by
James 3:13	his deeds in the gentleness of	wisdom	.
James 3:15	This	wisdom	is not that which comes down from
James 3:17	But the	wisdom	from above is first pure, then

Study:

🔍 *Wisdom* is another one of those words that appears only in a few places, but the concept behind it is a major thrust of the letter. James knows that Godly wisdom is the thing we lack when we don't handle the ebbs and flows of this life appropriately. The word itself debuts in James 1:5 and has a continued contextual contribution all the way to the end of the book. Watch for those instances where James doesn't use the word itself, but still urges his readers to be *wise*.

🔍 Definition of *wisdom* (*sophia*):

🔍 The next four uses of *wisdom* are found between 3:13-18. Here, James contrasts the "wisdom from above" with the wisdom that is not from above – the wisdom of the world. Even if you don't wish to define all the adjectives in this passage (i.e. *earthly, natural, demonic...pure, peaceable, gentle*, etc.), you may find it useful to mark them in a contrasting way and take some notes regarding these opposing *wisdoms*.

Characteristics of *wisdom from above*:

_____
_____
_____
_____
_____

Marked: ☐   My Mark:

Characteristics of *wisdom NOT from above*:

_____
_____
_____
_____
_____

Marked: ☐   My Mark:

Question:

📖 How would you summarize God's *wisdom* that comes from above?

_____
_____
_____

📖 How would you summarize the *wisdom* of the world?

_____
_____
_____
_____

📖 What do you suppose it is about the world's *wisdom* that is so alluring to mankind? Have you ever found yourself caught up in some of these devices? (i.e. bitter jealousy, selfish ambition, etc.)

Notes:

OPTIONAL WORDS

Remember that Optional Words are those words that are of some interest but may not be marked for a few different reasons: (1) they may not be exceedingly theologically significant, (2) they may be used so frequently that to mark them would mean making your Bible pages extremely crowded or too busy to focus on the other words marked, or (3) they may just be synonyms to the key words. It is up to your discretion whether or not to mark these words. Should you choose to mark any or all of these words, a Biblical concordance can help you find their occurrences in the original language.

WORD	TRANSLITERATION	OCC...	SUGGESTED SYMBOL	MARKED
God	*theos*	16	God (yellow triangle)	☐
Lord	*kyrios*	14	Lord (inverted triangle)	☐
Gives	*didōmi*	8	Gives (gift bow)	☐
Righteousness	*dikē*	8	Righteousness (blue oval)	☐
Trials	*peira*	7	Trials (red underline)	☐

My Mark:	My Mark:

My Mark:	My Mark:

My Mark:	My Mark:

Notes:

KEY CONCLUSIONS

THEME OF JAMES:

MAJOR TOPICS IN JAMES:

APPLICATIONS FROM JAMES:

MY KEY WORDS

If you found some words that you think are key to the text but are not listed, list them below and assign them a symbol if you wish!

WORD	CHAPTER(S)	OCCURRENCES	SYMBOL	MARKED
				☐
				☐
				☐
				☐
				☐
				☐
				☐
				☐
				☐
				☐
				☐
				☐
				☐
				☐

"keep yourselves in the love of God, waiting anxiously for the mercy of our Lord Jesus Christ to eternal life."

Jude 21

THE EPISTLE OF JUDE

STUDYING JUDE

1. Read the introduction to one of these guides at least once.
2. Read the "General Information" page to orient yourself to Jude's epistle.
3. Read Jude all the way through several times to familiarize yourself with the text.
4. Follow the directions found under "Key Concepts." This section will have you mark other important things prior to keywording the book.
5. Keyword the book:
   a. Turn to the first keywording page (e.g. *Jesus*) and locate the suggested symbol for that particular word.
   b. Use the reference list provided in order to locate the English words in your Bible that correspond to their respective Greek word.
   c. Mark the located word with the suggested symbol. Do this for all the key words provided in each guide.
   d. When applicable, answer the questions and/or follow the study prompts included for the words.
   e. For an even deeper study of the word, define it using a reputable Bible dictionary.
6. Mark the Optional Words at your own discretion using the suggested symbols or by creating your own.
7. Complete the "Key Conclusions" section.
8. Utilize the "My Key Words" section when applicable.

GENERAL INFORMATION

AUTHOR JUDE
The brother of Jesus & James
(cf. Matt. 13:55; Mark 6:3; Jude 1)

GENRE GENERAL EPISTLE

DATE c. 69 A.D.

WRITTEN FR. JERUSALEM

RECIPIENTS TO THOSE WHO ARE THE CALLED, BELOVED IN GOD THE FATHER, AND KEPT FOR JESUS CHRIST (Jude 1)
Likely the same Christian communities that Peter wrote to given very similar circumstances and timing.

OCCASION It's obvious from his language that Jude knows his readers and loves them dearly. He said in verse 3 that he desired to write to them about "our common salvation" – a supportive and encouraging message to be sure. That message, however, would have to wait. It seems that news reached him regarding false teachers causing problems for these Christians. What follows is one of the most scathing rebukes of false teachers in all the Bible.

KEY CONCEPTS

JUDE - THE OTHER BROTHER

Jude's name is a shortened form of Judas (*Ioudas*) and has an undertone meaning of being "renowned" or "famous." This is somewhat ironic, given that Jude is not found in the foreground of the early church nearly as much as his older brother, James – let alone his oldest brother, Jesus. Jude is either Jesus' youngest or second youngest brother, as Matthew lists him fourth while Mark lists him third in succession (cf. Matthew 13:55; Mark 6:3). Like James, Jude had his own struggles believing that Jesus was who He said He was, and he is included with Jesus' other unbelieving brothers (cf. John 7:1-9). But unlike James, Jude is not named as one of those who saw the risen Christ – though he may have accompanied some of the groups or individuals that did. Whenever his moment of clarity occurred, Jude eventually came around and fought for the faith set down by his brother, giving himself as "a bond-servant of Jesus Christ" (Jude 1).

DATE	VERSE	EVENT
A.D. 17	1 Corinthians 9:5	Jude is either married by this time or close to being so – Approximately 17-18 years old.
A.D. 26	John 2:12	Jesus' brothers, including Jude, are with Him at the feast in Cana.
A.D. 27	Matthew 13:55; Mark 6:3	Jesus' last visit to Nazareth – Jude listed as one of His brothers. He's listed third in Mark – fourth in Matthew.
A.D. 29	John 7:1-9	Jesus' brothers, including Jude, still don't believe in Him.
A.D. 30	Acts 1:13-14	Jesus' brothers are listed as having been in the upper room after His ascension.
/	/	Like James, Jude probably stayed in Jerusalem except for occasional travels for mission work (cf. 1 Cor. 9:5).
A.D. 69	Jude 1	**JUDE AUTHORS HIS EPISTLE**

PURPOSE STATEMENT

Jude leaves no question as to why he writes his letter. In verse 3, he states his initial intention of writing about "our common salvation," but ultimately redirects his pen to instruct his readers to "contend earnestly for the faith which was once for all handed down to the saints." False teachers have slithered their way into the ranks of God's people, but Jude isn't about to let them inject the poison of ungodliness and rebellion. An upbeat, encouraging message about salvation is always a wonderful thing, but the Lord's brother sees the "necessity" to sound the alarm and make sure that his fellow Christians are ready to fight for the established faith. God's truth has been handed down once for all – far be it from any man to meddle with the message!

> "Beloved, while I was making every effort to write to you about our common salvation, I felt the necessity to write to you appealing that you contend earnestly for the faith which was once for all handed down to the saints."
> – Jude 3

Suggestion: Lightly underline this verse using a distinct color. (Orange?)

Marked: ☐   **My Mark:**

Study:

- 🔍 Definition of *contend* (*epagōnizomai*):

- 🔍 If you'd like, mark *faith* (*pisteuō*) in verses 3, 5 (*believe*), & 20 (See "Optional Words" for a symbol suggestion.)

- 🔍 *Once for all* (*hapax* – 3, 5) and *handed down* (*paradidōmi* – 3) are also words of great interest. (See "Optional Words".) If you'd like, look these words up in your Bible dictionary too and consider what Jude is really saying here. What does it mean that THE faith was ONCE for all handed down?

Notes:

PETITION VERBS

Jude employs two petition verbs to focus his reader's minds on what they absolutely must know and do. He *appeals* to them – urging them to contend for the faith, and he *desires*, or wishes greatly, that they would be reminded of lessons learned from others' disobedience in the past. These types of words are strong indicators of a Bible writer's purposes for writing. It is no coincidence that *appealing* (*parakaleō*) is found in Jude's purpose statement and that his *desire* (*boulomai*) to remind them of important information is also expressed shortly thereafter.

PETITION VERBS	REFERENCE	GREEK	TRANSLITERATION
APPEALING	Jude 3	παρακαλέω	*parakaleō*
DESIRE	Jude 5	βούλομαι	*boulomai*

Suggestion: Mark these words with a distinct symbol.

Marked: ☐   My Mark:

Notes:

IMPERATIVES

The bulk of Jude's letter is a description and denunciation of the false teachers who have wormed their way into the church. That being the case, his instructions for his readers are simple: (1) don't get swept away with these guys, and (2) help them if you can. Only five imperative verbs are used to convey these instructions. If you'd like, use your mark for imperatives to identify them in the text.

CAUTION: As with James, there could be some symbol confusion depending how you mark the imperatives in Jude. *Love* (or *beloved*), *mercy*, *God*, and *keep* (or *kept*) are key words, and *save* is an optional word. Keep these words in mind should you choose to mark them.

My Mark - IMPERATIVES: ☐

IMPERATIVES	REFERENCE
"REMEMBER THE WORDS"	Jude 17
"KEEP YOURSELVES IN THE LOVE OF GOD"	Jude 21
"HAVE MERCY ON SOME"	Jude 22
"SAVE OTHERS"	Jude 23
"AND ON SOME HAVE MERCY WITH FEAR"	Jude 23

Notes:

JUDE & II PETER

While critics try to disparage the letters of Jude and 2 Peter due to their similarities, an actual comparison of their contents is incredibly faith affirming. The most likely timeline of composition puts Peter's second letter having been written around A.D. 67 and Jude's at A.D. 69. Peter writes to his audience regarding dangers of false teachers who will "secretly introduce destructive heresies" in the near future (2 Peter 2:1); whereas Jude affirms to the same groups of people that this exact thing has already happened (Jude 4). Note the future tense in Peter's letter and how Jude employs the past tense. Peter warned of coming danger while Jude made absolutely sure that these churches knew that the danger was now in their midst. If you'd like, compare the verses below and note some of their similarities.

JUDE	2 PETER	SIMILARITIES
4	2:1	
4	2:3	
6	2:4	
7	2:6	
8	2:10	
9	2:11	
10	2:12	
11	2:15	
12	2:13	
12	2:17	
13	2:17	
16	2:18	
17	3:2	
18	3:3	

Notes:

TRIPLETS IN JUDE

Another interesting literary feature of Jude's letter is that of his use of triplets (or triads). It seems that Jude found the pattern of threes to be a useful communication tool. Scholars have varied opinions as to why Jude chooses to employ this beautiful method, but it's this author's humble opinion that things just seem more aesthetic and powerful in threes. Notice some of the types of triplets Jude uses – his lofty description of Christians as "called," "beloved," and "kept" in verse 2; sobering warnings from the examples of Cain, Balaam, and Korah in verse 11; and of course, the Father, Son, and Holy Spirit in verses 20-21. If you'd like, mark these triplets in a distinctive way in the text to spotlight Jude's distinctive style. (See the marking suggestion below the chart.) Use the blank spaces in the chart to add any other triplets you may identify and want to include.

TRIPLET	REFERENCE	MARKED
Jude – Bond Servant – Brother	1	☐
Called – Beloved – Kept	1	☐
Mercy – Peace – Love	2	☐
Condemned – Ungodly – Deny Christ	4	☐
People saved from Egypt – Angels – Sodom & Gomorrah	5-7	☐
Defile the Flesh – Reject Authority – Revile Angels	8	☐
Way of Cain – Error of Balaam – Rebellion of Korah	11	☐
Execute Judgment – Convict Deeds – Convict Words	15	☐
Grumblers – Follow Lusts – Speak Arrogantly	16	☐
Cause Divisions – Worldly-Minded – Devoid of the Spirit	19	☐
Building – Praying – Waiting	20-21	☐
Holy Spirit – God – Lord Jesus Christ	20-21	☐
Mercy on doubters – Save others – Mercy on others	22-23	☐
Before all time – Now – Forever	25	☐
		☐
		☐
		☐

Suggestion: Write a superscript 1, 2, & 3 near the triplets above.
Example: ^{1}Mercy ^{2}Peace ^{3}Love

Marked: ☐   **My Mark:**

Study:

🔍 There are at least two other lists in Jude's letter that are not triplets.

Verses 12-13 contain five negative descriptions of the false teachers: (1) *hidden reefs*, (2) *clouds without water*, (3) *dead and uprooted autumn trees*, (4) *wild waves*, & (5) *wandering stars*.

Marked: ☐   **My Mark:**

Verse 25 lists four praises for God: (1) *glory*, (2) *majesty*, (3) *dominion*, & (4) *authority*.

Marked: ☐   **My Mark:**

Notes:

JEWISH NATURE OF THE LETTER

It is abundantly clear that Jude wrote to the same Christian communities that Peter did. 1 Peter 1:1 indicates that these groups were "scattered throughout Pontus, Galatia, Cappadocia, Asia, and Bithynia." A survey study of events in the New Testament will reveal that these Christian groups had a strong representation of both Jews and Gentiles. Jews from some of these areas were present in Jerusalem on the day of Pentecost (Acts 2:9-11), which makes it probable that these new converts took the Gospel back home with them. And a consideration of Paul's missionary journeys shows us that he and his companions also established churches in these areas (cf. Acts 16:6; 18:23; 19:10, 26). That being said, it seems that Jude has an expectation that his readers are familiar with the Old Testament given the quantity of references he makes to it. Like you did in James, you may want to draw a symbol in your margin or on the word itself when you come to references in the Old Testament. See the symbol suggestion below the chart.

VERSE	NAME/SUBJECT	MARKED
5	Land of Egypt	☐
6	Angels	☐
7	Sodom and Gomorrah	☐
9	Michael the Archangel	☐
9	Moses	☐
11	Cain	☐
11	Balaam	☐
11	Korah	☐
14	Enoch	☐
14	Adam	☐

Suggestion: Draw a symbol on these terms or in the margin of the verses. (✡ ?)

Marked: ☐   **My Mark:**

Notes:

KEY WORDS

JESUS

Excluding pronouns, Jude mentions Jesus by name seven times in his twenty-five-verse letter. Now that's what we call a key word! With the staggering amount of condemnation for those who are turning "the grace of our God into licentiousness" and denying "our only Master and Lord, Jesus Christ" (v.4), it only makes sense that Jude constantly namedrops Him to impress the point on his readers that Jesus is still the answer. He's the one who has true "glory, majesty, dominion and authority" (v.25). Look for and mark the "deity words" in Jude's epistle: *Jesus Christ, Lord, God, & Holy Spirit*. Decide how you want to mark these words before beginning, as there is some variety in how Jude writes. (See below for some suggestions.) Take note under the "Study" section that there are also several optional words you may want to mark that are related to the "deity words."

WORD	GREEK-L	TRANSLITERATION	OCCURRENCES	SUGGESTED SYMBOL
Jesus	Ἰησοῦς	*Iēsous*	7	Jesus

Jesus Christ   Lord Jesus Christ   Lord (by itself)

Marked: ☐   **My Mark:**

Jude 1	Jude, a bond-servant of	Jesus	Christ, and brother of James, To
Jude 1	in God the Father, and kept for	Jesus	Christ:
Jude 4	deny our only Master and Lord,	Jesus	Christ.
Jude 5	all things once for all, that the	Lord	, after saving a people out of the
Jude 17	by the apostles of our Lord	Jesus	Christ,
Jude 21	for the mercy of our Lord	Jesus	Christ to eternal life.
Jude 25	the only God our Savior, through	Jesus	Christ our Lord, *be* glory,

WORD	GREEK-R	TRANSLITERATION	OCCURRENCES	SUGGESTED SYMBOL
Lord	κυριος	*kyrios*	7	Lord

Marked: ☐   **My Mark:**

Jude 4	and deny our only Master and	Lord	, Jesus Christ.

Jude 8	defile the flesh, and reject	authority	, and revile angelic majesties.
Jude 9	railing judgment, but said, "The	Lord	rebuke you!"
Jude 14	prophesied, saying, "Behold, the	Lord	came with many thousands of His
Jude 17	beforehand by the apostles of our	Lord	Jesus Christ,
Jude 21	anxiously for the mercy of our	Lord	Jesus Christ to eternal life.
Jude 25	Savior, through Jesus Christ our	Lord	, *be* glory, majesty, dominion and

WORD	GREEK-L	TRANSLITERATION	OCCURRENCES	SUGGESTED SYMBOL
God	θεός	*theos*	4	G͟o͟d͟ (triangle)

Marked: ☐   **My Mark:**

Jude 1	who are the called, beloved in	God	the Father, and kept for Jesus
Jude 4	persons who turn the grace of our	God	into licentiousness and deny our
Jude 21	keep yourselves in the love of	God	, waiting anxiously for the mercy
Jude 25	to the only	God	our Savior, through Jesus Christ

WORD	GREEK	TRANSLITERATION	OCC…	SUGGESTED SYMBOL
Holy Spirit	ἁγίῳ πνεύματι	*hagiō pneumati*	2	Holy Spirit (cloud)

Marked: ☐   **My Mark:**

Jude 19	worldly-minded, devoid of the	Spirit	.
Jude 20	holy faith, praying in the	Holy Spirit	,

Study:

🔍 You probably noticed that the English word *Lord* occurs in the same list as *Jesus* in verse 5. This is not a mistake, since the actual Greek term there is *Jesus* (*Iēsous*). Whether you mark it as *Jesus* or *Lord*, it will be appropriate either way.

🔍 If you'd like, mark the pronouns related to deity in Jude's letter (e.g. "He" in verse 6). Be sure to doublecheck the context so that you assign the correct deity symbol to its corresponding pronoun.

Marked: ☐   **My Mark:**

🔍 With all the false teaching about God and His nature spreading through these churches, Jude uses a word that solidifies for his readers the fact that they are indeed serving the one true God. That word is *only* (*monos*) in verses 4 and 25. If you'd like, mark this word in a distinctive way (see "Optional Words" for a symbol suggestion) and define it.

Definition of *monos*:

Marked: ☐   **My Mark:**

Question:

📖 What other words in the text indicate the nature and power of the Father, Son, and Spirit? See verses 24-25 for some good ones. (Note: *authority* in verse 25 is a different Greek word than *authority* in verse 8, but you may want to mark it the same way given the subject matter.)

📖 Aside from assuring his readers that they serve a God who has higher standards for them than the false teachers, why else do you think Jude includes so much deity terminology? Is he trying to comfort them? Motivate them?

📖 What, if anything, has changed or enhanced your perspective of God by marking the terms in this section?

Notes:

BELOVED

Jude loves the Christians he writes to. One can almost feel the intensity and urgency with which he writes to this group as he does not want to see any harm come to them. His description of *beloved* for his readers is a striking contrast to those "certain persons" (v.4) that he is about to deal with. It's a scary thing to think of someone harming those whom you love – especially spiritually. That is why Jude admonishes them, saying, "keep yourselves in the love of God, waiting anxiously for the mercy of our Lord Jesus Christ to eternal life" (v.21).

WORD	GREEK-R	TRANSLITERATION	OCCURRENCES	SUGGESTED SYMBOL
Love	αγαπαω	*agapaō*	7	L♥ve

Marked: ☐   **My Mark:**

Jude 1	To those who are the called,	beloved	in God the Father, and kept for
Jude 2	May mercy and peace and	love	be multiplied to you.
Jude 3		Beloved	, while I was making every effort
Jude 12	men who are hidden reefs in your	love	feasts when they feast with you
Jude 17	But you,	beloved	, ought to remember the words that
Jude 20	But you,	beloved	, building yourselves up on your
Jude 21	keep yourselves in the	love	of God, waiting anxiously for the

Question:

📖 How would you summarize the main instructions that Jude gives to those whom he calls *beloved*?

📖 What lessons can we learn from Jude regarding our *love* for other Christians? How about our *love* for those still lost in the world?

📖 What else caught your attention regarding the way Jude writes about *love*?

Notes:

UNGODLY

Everything a righteous person is, an *ungodly* person is not. Jude describes the false teachers among his readers in many negative ways, but *ungodly* is the term he uses the most – perhaps because it is simply the best description of their existence. This word (*sebō*) holds the idea of being wicked, profane, sacrilegious, and ultimately that which stands against God. Although Jude does not discuss the fine details of what these people were teaching, it was depraved and dangerous enough for him to issue one of the strongest condemnations in all the Bible against leading God's people in error. Jude is just getting warmed up in verse 4 with his first declaration of *ungodliness* in these teachers' lives.

WORD	GREEK-R	TRANSLITERATION	OCCURRENCES	SUGGESTED SYMBOL
Ungodly	σεβω	*sebō*	6	Ungodly

Marked: ☐   **My Mark:**

Jude 4	marked out for this condemnation,	ungodly	persons who turn the grace of our
Jude 15	upon all, and to convict all the	ungodly	of all their ungodly deeds which
Jude 15	all the ungodly of all their	ungodly	deeds which they have done in an
Jude 15	which they have done in an	ungodly	way, and of all the
Jude 15	and of all the harsh things which	ungodly	sinners have spoken against Him."
Jude 18	following after their own	ungodly	lusts."

Study:

🔍 *Ungodly* seems to be Jude's baseline term to describe the false teachers. As mentioned above, he has a wide array of descriptions of these guys and what they do. After you mark *ungodly* in your Bible, go back through the letter and identify these other actions and descriptions. You may want to shade these descriptions with a color of your choice or simply list them below.

CAUTION: This will be a very important list-set to have available. However, you may want to come back to this section after you have keyworded the rest of the book so that your shading does not accidentally overlap your other symbols in these verses.

Examples: *licentiousness / deny our only Master* (v.4) –
    cause divisions / worldly-minded / devoid of the Spirit (v.19) – etc.

Marked: ☐   **My Mark:**

Actions and Descriptions of the false teachers:

🔍 Now that you have listed and/or marked the descriptions and actions of the false teachers, begin thinking in terms of the *results* of those actions. Under *judgment*, the next key word, you'll record and/or mark the consequences of these rebellious behaviors.

Question:

📖 In verses 5-7, Jude lists the people who were rescued from Egypt, angels who left their proper domain, and the inhabitants of Sodom and Gomorrah as those who are "exhibited as an example in undergoing the punishment of eternal fire." Which of these examples resonates with you the most? The fact that people who witnessed miracles forgot so quickly? That even angels, some of God's closest associates, could turn from the blessings they had in hand? Or that a city could be so wicked that not even ten righteous people could be found in it? (cf. Genesis 18:26-33)

📖 In verse 11, Jude says that the false teachers have "gone the way of Cain," "rushed headlong into the error of Balaam," and "perished in the rebellion of Korah." Go back to the Old Testament and refresh your memory of these accounts. What lessons can we learn from these people of old and how do their stories apply to Jude's letter?

The way of Cain (cf. Genesis 4; Hebrews 11:4; 1 John 3:12):

The error of Balaam (Numbers 22-24; 31:8, 16):

The rebellion of Korah (Numbers 16; 26:9-11):

📖 Consider Jude's five illustrations from nature in verses 12-13. Describe the dangers and uselessness of these things.

📖 Which descriptions or actions of the false teachers stand out to you as particularly evil and despicable? What makes them so?

📖 How would you summarize what these false teachers are doing (or trying to do) by creeping into the church unnoticed? How does Jude say they are accomplishing this? (cf. v.16).

📖 What do these *ungodly* people stand to gain by gaining an audience in the Lord's church?

📖 Have you ever encountered or had to deal with someone in the church who shared some characteristics of these false teachers? How was the situation handled? What was the end result?

Notes:

JUDGMENT

It doesn't take long while reading Jude's letter to realize why he speaks of *judgment* the way he does. We serve a loving and gracious God, but living a life in open denial and opposition to His Son, Jesus Christ, will find us on the wrong side of the "judgment of the great day" (v.6). Just as ungodliness is Jude's warmup to describe what these false teachers are guilty of, so *judgment* is Jude's prelude to describing the destruction, fire, and darkness that awaits them because of that ungodliness. As you read Jude's letter, watch for the terrifying consequences awaiting those who deny Christ, live debaucherously, and assail God's beloved people.

WORD	GREEK-R	TRANSLITERATION	OCCURRENCES	SUGGESTED SYMBOL
Judgment	κρινω	*krinō*	6	Judgment

Marked: ☐   **My Mark:**

Jude 4	marked out for this	condemnation	, ungodly persons who turn
Jude 6	bonds under darkness for the	judgment	of the great day,
Jude 9	Michael the archangel, when he	disputed	with the devil and argued
Jude 9	pronounce against him a railing	judgment	, but said, "The Lord rebuke
Jude 15	to execute	judgment	upon all, and to convict all
Jude 22	have mercy on some, who are	doubting	;

Study:

🔍 If you'd like, mark *convict* (*elenchō*) in verse 15 with a similar symbol as it is related in meaning to *judgment*.

Marked: ☐   **My Mark:**

🔍 Just as you made a list and/or marked the descriptions and actions of the false teachers under *ungodly*, it's equally important to the study of Jude's letter to understand the *results* of ungodliness. After you mark *judgment*, go back through the letter and identify the words and phrases that indicate the punishments these wicked people will receive. You can either list them below, mark them distinctively in the text (**suggestion**: red squiggly line), or do both.

CAUTION: The same marking principle applies here as it did when marking the actions and descriptions of the false teachers under *ungodly*. You may want to come back to this section after you have keyworded the rest of the book so that your mark (red squiggly line?) does not overlap your other symbols in these verses.

Examples: *destroyed (v.5) – eternal bonds under darkness (v.6) –*
punishment of eternal fire (v.7) – etc.

Marked: ☐　　　　**My Mark:**

Results of living ungodly:

Question:

- According to Jude 9, do God's archangels have the authority to pronounce *judgment*? What was Michael's response in this situation? What lesson is there for us in this?

- Eternal fire and eternal darkness are both listed as punishments for those who live corruptly as the false teachers did. How would you reconcile fire (that which we understand to produce light) coinciding with a place of darkness? (cf. Matthew 5:22; 8:12; 13:42; 25:30).

📖 Should a Christian's motive for behaving righteously be the fear of *judgment*? Why or why not? What do you think motivated Jude's readers to keep contending for the faith?

Notes:

ETERNAL

Jude discusses the *eternal* as a double-edged sword. On one hand, the rebellious soul can expect "the punishment of eternal fire" (v.7) and black darkness that "has been reserved forever" (v.13). On the other hand, those who "contend earnestly for the faith" (v.3) and keep themselves "in the love of God" (v.21) will inherit eternal life. Jude knows that these Christians' forever home is at stake. Should the false teachers command an influence over these peoples' lives, their eternity will be lost. Eternality in and of itself is a baffling concept. What's more is how an eternal Creator, who is "before all time and now and forever" (v.25), loves us so much that He is willing to *spare* us what we truly deserve and have *mercy* on us who believe through His Son, Jesus Christ.

WORD	GREEK-R	TRANSLITERATION	OCCURRENCES	SUGGESTED SYMBOL
Eternal	αιων	*aiōn*	5	‹Eternal›

Marked: ☐   **My Mark:**

Jude 7	in undergoing the punishment of	eternal	fire.
Jude 13	black darkness has been reserved	forever	.
Jude 21	mercy of our Lord Jesus Christ to	eternal	life.
Jude 25	and authority,	before all time	and now and forever. Amen.
Jude 25	before all time and now and	forever	. Amen.

Study:

🔍 Mark *eternal* (*aidios*) in verse 6 with the same symbol as it is synonymous with *aiōn*.

Marked: ☐   **My Mark:**

Question:

📖 Some today believe that upon their deaths, they will simply cease to exist – that God would never allow a person who didn't want to know Him to be punished forever. Do you think Jude means *eternal* metaphorically when it comes to punishment?

📖 What do you think Jude's objective is in speaking of the *eternal* five times in his twenty-five verse letter?

Notes:

KEPT

Like eternality, the concept of *kept* in Jude's letter is either the most wonderful thing in the world or the thing to be feared most. *Kept* (*tēreō*) conveys the idea of something or someone being watched and/or guarded. The contrast is clear. The ungodly have a reservation with torment – being held "in eternal bonds under darkness" (v.6). The saints have a date with destiny – being held and guarded in the loving arms of our Heavenly Father. Make no mistake…God's people have a reservation indeed. "In my Father's house are many dwelling places; if it were not so, I would have told you; for I go to prepare a place for you" (John 14:2).

WORD	GREEK-L	TRANSLITERATION	OCCURRENCES	SUGGESTED SYMBOL
Kept	τηρέω	tēreō	5	(Kept)

Marked: ☐

My Mark:

Jude 1	beloved in God the Father, and	kept	for Jesus Christ:
Jude 6	And angels who did not	keep	their own domain, but abandoned
Jude 6	their proper abode, He has	kept	in eternal bonds under darkness
Jude 13	whom the black darkness has been	reserved	forever.
Jude 21		keep	yourselves in the love of God,

Question:

📖 In verse one, *kept* is a passive verb, meaning that Jesus is doing the keeping of "those who are called." In verse 21, *keep* is an imperative, meaning that it's *our* responsibility to *keep* ourselves in the love of God. How would you explain what Jude is saying here?

📖 Read 1 Peter 1:3-5. How does Peter's use of *reserved* (*tēreō*) strengthen your understanding of what God has in store for us?

📖 What other lessons can we learn from those who do not *keep* or watch over what they have (v.6)? Can you think of any other examples in the Bible of individuals losing what was already theirs?

Notes:

MERCY

Jesus said, "Be merciful, just as your Father is merciful" (Luke 6:36). An incredible demand from an incredible Savior. Not surprisingly, James echoes Jesus' words by stating, "For judgment will be merciless to one who has shown no mercy; mercy triumphs over judgment" (James 2:13). And their little brother, Jude, brings it all home. Though surrounded by carnal, rebellious liars, Jude tells his readers to dig deep and have *mercy* on these people (vss. 22-23). It's going to take forgiveness, patience, and maturity to win these lost souls back to the Lord, but Jude calls their attention to why they should try – because the Lord has offered *them* mercy. What a beautiful lesson we can learn from such a short letter. We don't deserve *mercy* either, but God still tries with us.

WORD	GREEK-R	TRANSLITERATION	OCCURRENCES	SUGGESTED SYMBOL
Mercy	ελεος	*eleos*	4	Mercy

Marked: ☐   **My Mark:**

Jude 2	May	mercy	and peace and love be multiplied
Jude 21	of God, waiting anxiously for the	mercy	of our Lord Jesus Christ to
Jude 22	And have	mercy	on some, who are doubting;
Jude 23	out of the fire; and on some have	mercy	with fear, hating even the garment

Study:

🔍 Definition of *mercy* (*eleos*):

___

🔍 Jude is very clear how his readers are supposed to have *mercy* on those around them. They must first understand that they themselves have received the *mercy* of God (vss. 2 & 21). And in light of this knowledge, they are to "save others, snatching them out of the fire" (vs. 23). You may want to mark *save* (*sōzō*) and *snatching* (*harpazō*) in your text (see "Optional Words" for symbol suggestions).

Save (*sōzō*): 3 (*salvation*), 5 (*saving*), 23 (*save*), 25 (*Savior*)

Marked: ☐   **My Mark:**

Snatching (harpazō): 23

Marked: ☐   **My Mark:**

🔍 You may have already guessed it by sounding out the word, but *harpazō* is related to the English word, harpoon. Define this word using your Bible dictionary and then consider this meaning in the context of saving souls out of the fire. What does the definition suggest about the urgency of soul-winning?

Definition of *harpazō*:

_____
_____

Question:

📖 In light of the definition of *mercy* and the contexts in which Jude uses it, what do you suppose it means to actually have *mercy* on someone?

_____
_____

📖 Go back and read the verses above from Jesus, James, and Jude. Why does God want us to show *mercy* to others?

_____
_____

📖 Why do we sometimes not show *mercy* to others?

_____
_____

📖 What actions or mindsets do you think will be helpful for you to show *mercy* to others in the future?

_____
_____

Notes:

_____
_____

OPTIONAL WORDS

WORD	TRANSLITERATION	OCC...	SUGGESTED SYMBOL	MARKED
Save	*sōzō*	4	Save (arrow)	☐
Faith	*pisteuō*	3	Faith (green box)	☐
Only	*monos*	2	Only (with 1)	☐
Once for all	*hapax*	2	Once for all (highlighted)	☐
Handed down	*paradidōmi*	1	Handed down (highlighted)	☐
Snatching	*harpazō*	1	Snatching (arrow)	☐

My Mark:	My Mark:
My Mark:	My Mark:
My Mark:	My Mark:

Notes:

KEY CONCLUSIONS

THEME OF JUDE:

MAJOR TOPICS IN JUDE:

APPLICATIONS FROM JUDE:

MY KEY WORDS

WORD	CHAPTER(S)	OCCURRENCES	SYMBOL	MARKED
				☐
				☐
				☐
				☐
				☐
				☐
				☐
				☐
				☐
				☐
				☐
				☐
				☐
				☐

www.ingramcontent.com/pod-product-compliance
Lightning Source LLC
Chambersburg PA
CBHW051357110526
44592CB00023B/2867